THE KING'S LIARS

Susan Gordon Byron

Parlyaree Press
Atlanta, Georgia
www.parlyaree.com

Copyright © 2026 by Susan Gordon Byron
All Rights Reserved
Printed locally; distributed globally.
First Edition, 2026

All rights reserved. This book or any portion thereof may not be reproduced or used in any manner whatsoever without the express written permission of the publisher except for the use of brief quotations in a book review.

Library of Congress Cataloging-in-Publication Data
Names: Byron, Susan Gordon, author.
Title: The King's Liars / Susan Gordon Byron
Description: First Edition | Atlanta : Parlyaree Press, 2026
Identifiers: LCCN: applied for | ISBN 9781961206274 (paperback)
Subjects: LCGFT: Poetry
LC record available at https://lccn.loc.gov/

Interior & Cover Design by Parlyaree Press

The Kings's Liars is typeset in Baskerville, Garamond, FindReplace, and Bookeye Sadie. Cover and Interior Imagery Licensed for use.

Print ISBN: 978-1-961206-27-4
Ebook ISBN: 978-1-961206-28-1

Advanced Praise for The King's Liars

"Susan Gordan Byron's *The King's Liars* uses elliptical, intimate, and surreal language to take the reader on a journey: From Medusa, Virginia Woolf, the history of the face cream, to A Streetcar Named Desire, the 'lyric I' destabilises and dazzles in various poetic forms. At the tug of private wars, possibilities abound beyond shrinking in silence and smashing things on purpose. To long for something else without knowing what it is makes us all tourists: 'It's your morning, too, yours a photogenic ripple'. Amidst mundanity, insights do not preclude hope: 'My favourite lie is the future / An unhandled punch of time / Sometimes called a daydream'. This book is for those who 'wandered out from under their eyes / and into the lane, coughing up ivy.'"

-Tim Tim Cheng
Author of *The Tattoo Collector*, Nine Arches Press

"Playful, strange and at times unsettling, *The King's Liars* offers a catalogue of uncanny happenings: a bedroom turning itself inside out; shoes so small 'they can hide in other shoes'; a thought made visible like a rope uncoiling.... But beneath the surrealism is an unspoken darkness, a 'bottled black quiet' of unanswered questions and kept secrets. Someone laughs at the wrong moments; words, and their meanings, get up to leave."

-Tom Bailey
Editor of *And Other Poems*

"Susan Gordon Byron's *The King's Liars* is filled with strange and wonderful acts of creation and reclamation: from sinister figures with ivy for eyes, to the bodies of slain emperors, to Medusa's desire to be 'filthy, heavy, rotten' against the men she turns to stone. These poems translate the everyday as eldritch fable, in lines full of fresh-minted images and phrases. A truly original debut."

-Jessica Traynor
Author of *New Arcana*, Bloodaxe Books

THE
KING'S
LIARS

To the tourists.

THE KING'S LIARS

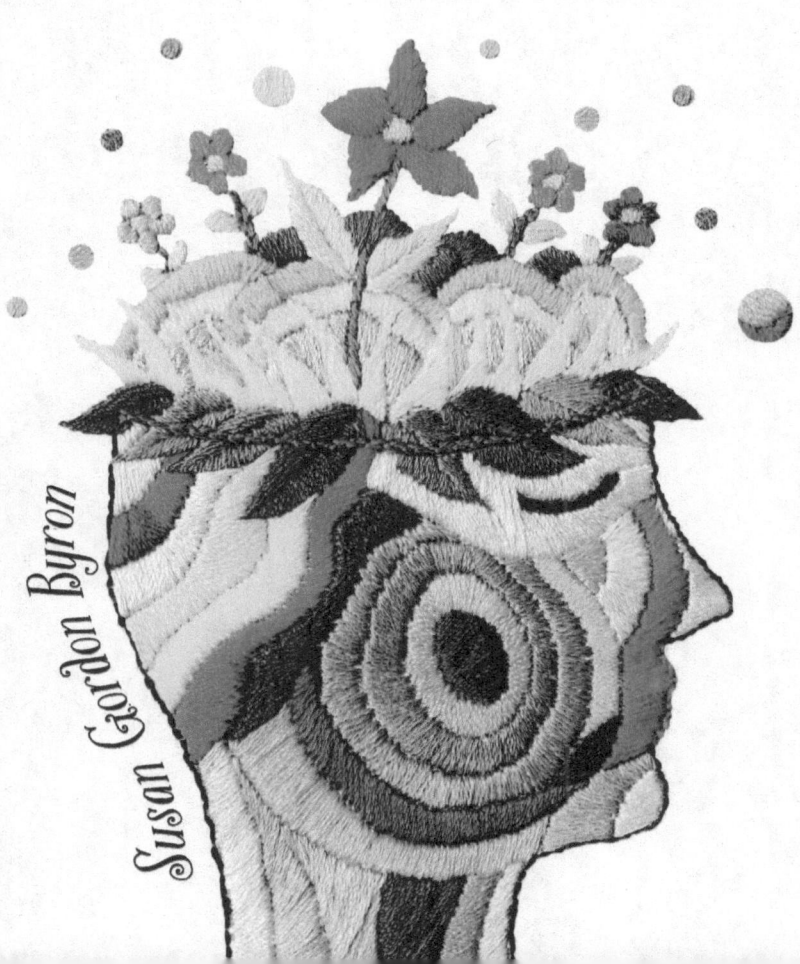

Susan Gordon Byron

TABLE OF CONTENTS

41 years old and reading Mr Men	1
When a Man Washes In	2
How to turn one villain into two	3
I've seen Mikaela	4
Medusa's Sonnet	5
beeps dashes and byes	6
Face cream	8
The teenager	9
Is it still my city?	10
Stupendous Ruler Painter	11
Rapper's SUV Mood	12
I'm sorry, Machiavelli	13
Psychiatrist and prisoner I	14
Psychiatrist and prisoner II	15
The Holiday	16
Cliff / Boy	17
Planet introduces herself	18
Bed rest	19
Cybernated	21
Midway through building a girl	23
paint the room yellow because	24
IRL	25
I suppose friends keep watch, too	26
Lethargy	27
Jealous	28

41 years old and reading Mr Men

I was shocked but more accepting than I should have been, by which I mean I did not ask why, because this was a dream. I lost my coat too, and what did that mean? An omen or warning, maybe. A black coat from Reiss.

It's your morning, too, yours a photogenic ripple. My morning twists on the spot. It's these questions I have

(an astral whodunnit: a whydreamit). So much chasing in dreams. One thing is missed and going unmissed. O to be so unexamined. Eyes open, and reason – unmissed and never called for – climbs in with speaking limbs. A chain. Then a snake. Sometimes a day.

When a Man Washes In

Okay, I'll keep it short,
because life is long and
my look at you is long—
I said I'd keep this short.
Your blue is long and
still leaking into mine.

How to turn one villain into two

Guests were advised not to go to their windows at night, so instead they imagined the man with ivy for eyes, an ill appetite, how he rode on horseback through Sussex, licked the hills dark and dry.

The young couple's skin was bare and soft; the hotel's five stars hard and bright. Pale under the stars, they sank into linen, fluffed egg whites, and marmalade. They were told what luxury was

while they sculpted nightmares: a new couple, who liked to drown clouds and nibble at hills. Who wandered out from under their eyes and into the lane, coughing up ivy. They came back for breakfast.

I've seen Mikaela

1. ignore every mantra.
2. sing in black.
3. sleep on a teenage beach.
4. slip from a hand.
5. enjoy concrete.
6. smear glass, while
7. muffled behind it, or
8. not a sound at all. a smell, Number
9. in a bottle.

I've seen Mikaela

10. shouting in dreams.
11. make sense of you.
12. making sense of you with a GIF.
13. wrestle with equations.
14. talk in spirals.
15. discover a word, otiose, and
16. know its meaning as it gets up to leave.
17. shrink from the unearned quiet,
18. a spineless quiet,
19. this spiny quiet.
20. a bottled black quiet.

Medusa's Sonnet

That was my face. The quietus. The shot.
Eyes were hot rings circling, falling free.
Remember my skin? Cold, pinholed by rot.
Lashes – kinky brooms to sweep the debris.
And who was the last man I turned to stone?
A music teacher, a violinist,

He fell across minims of flesh and bone.
Now I ask, was it then, was I richest
In a deep red sweater, and winter skin?

I counted Nutcrackers; and I felt poor;
Travel without leaving the room I'm in;
The novels I did not know. I am sure,
It's decided, I'll go back to stone men:
I'll be filthy, heavy, rotten again.

beeps dashes and byes

Her messages are balloons
striping
through
a wage.

From 9 to 5 a bubbling sonnet
beeps
and
pops

filled with dash dot
dot
alert
love.

The love is frowning.
Love
has a
thermometer.

xx love
Love's favourite letter
is
x.

He's in the chrome hollows
between
beeps and
dots.

The hollows are deep
until
they're
not.

I don't dash dash
alert
you
anymore.

Let me go.
Beep
is
inefficient.

Beep is so
long, it's
virtually
a death.

Vibrate and rattle:
beep
must
die.

Power down.
Blue to
empty
bye.

Bip is better than beep.
We'll say
dash bye
faster.

Dash bip bip
bye is
properly
living.

Face cream

You know it by its tagline, its scent.
It's what your mother had on her dressing room table.
The first bottle was a gift from a former chemist to his wife. Did she
    tell him?
They said I'm not breathing but I feel fine.
Is my skin too blue? Fine. I laugh in the wrong places. Fine.
Your friends talk and I miss the beat. Okay.
I've become a piccolo.

Half a flute.
Don't you dare say *piercing*.
A cry in the slowest motion. A lone peal
pasted in a Sunday night Tudor drama of Cromwellian mutters and
    candles.
The pages beneath my brows are not creased. They're fine.
Always fine. My body is small.
I got lost in a cupboard.

When they first met,
She was cool water, orange
and gin poured into the chemist's goblet.
This was before the smashed mirror. Before he threatened to wear
    earplugs.
She smashed it on purpose. Does he know that?
His calculations were, he thought, expert,
but did she keep the space between here and here to herself?

Oil of Olay has stated that 'The first bottle of Oil of Olay
was a gift from a former chemist to his wife'.

The teenager

pretends to sleep through
flaps of laughter that die in flight,
shouts announcing nothing,
and a bedroom turning itself inside out

trying to figure out why
the wardrobe calls out about
this girl's height. 'Short!'
and making short doubtful.

The girl turns on her side
for more from outside.
A guy on the side of a bus:
his poster slapped on one side of a bus.

Another face stretching into meaning,
part of the plot in this private war.
Branded trainers climb from a drawer:
there's a stadium in the name she paid for.

The room has finished its reversing.
Still insufficient, but still
something, and in the something
she takes an older day

from retirement. The dull army
of afternoons, but there
was that time with Marlon in Streetcar.
And Whitman, who

left his leaves everywhere.
She and a stadium of pretenders,
not old enough to know
the honesty she's found.

Is it still my city?

Yes. If you make it thick.
A fog, thick; the wills, thick;
an owl's stare, thick.

The bookseller smiled.

'You, too?' Snared by a
lawyer, Jaggers, top hats,
titles, and seedy little shops.

The stories stagger on.
There's no real stop.
And I hear a cute, moneyed
street pleading.

Its tears are trapped under
layers of polish. Remember
the real? The desert's healing?

Impulse wakens and gnaws.
I look again to a place
I don't remember, back then.

Stupendous Ruler Painter

after David Hockney's A Bigger Splash (1967)

Say sorry to a silver totem. Not to make it to the
Tate Modern in ten years; may as well be a century.

It's Sunday morning, and I pull a silver hair from my head.
Your masterpiece small on a wall back there.

A smell only smelling in memory. Not a masterpiece,
I decide, just that you were the first, being very old now.

I accept the bitterness of youth: A useful lemon bitterness.
So many silver days clamped to a canvas. A bigger splash:

There being no bodies makes me think intensely of bodies.
Skin must be conjured, an orbit of silver days across it.

I hear a tune, and it's the Beatles, a silver orbit measured in days.
This. Desire, and the later-born audit of desire.

Rapper's SUV Mood

Rubbish flapping on concrete.
The things you say.

A pavement preserving jam
and jarring it behind my eyes.

Thank god you can't see
the traffic under there.

I'm sorry, Machiavelli

Reduced to an oilish flame
in the scented dark.
I'm too bold and new to see you:
of the moment, relevant,
but the *zeit* is, after all, parochial.
If you could look back,
you'd meet a watery glare—want, as spark—
cleverness as Catherine wheel—
a headache combed out. Body, as wax.
A constellation
in gloved hands.
If you can see me, Mack, I might ask you
for a calculation. Why is the sum of all this
no more than heat leaking from a blur?

Psychiatrist with prisoner I
after Dr Gwen Adshead's The Devil You Know

A room sits in your throat.

A man sits in the room.
My tiger, it's all routine:
claws retracted on both sides

Faded stripes on both sides
Your metal, scrubbed in
Behind the eyes.

This animal,
Poured out like a jug,
Long before me,

Now logically empty.
Nothing is said, and
It's the opposite of choking.

One day, you start to talk.
I worry in a mirror & pop
out the other side.

Psychiatrist with prisoner II

The graduate did not want a plastic future, Benjamin Braddick
    said it,
yet we have it. The chairs are plastic. The floor. Her security pass,
    pen and watchstrap.
All are practical, hard, enduring. A triad of qualities equalling
    an infliction.
The surfaces are too apt to describe, but they are mean.
The prisoner is going on a bit; he endures, too.
She remembers the books that got her there; a cascade of
    theories and terms;
her confidence meeting them: the plasticity she had.
The other voice unmuffles. She must herd a professional's reply.
'What do you think of, when I say "plasticity?"' He repeats the word.
He is thinking visibly,
it's like watching a rope uncoil. The silence draws lines around
    her muscles.
'Placid,' he decides. 'A sea calm.'

The Holiday

Lucky you. Your awe is fresh to you, like a palm reading,
and your glowing self equal to it. Belief in your glow, equal to it.

You are the adventure. Offered a place at RADA you didn't take,
your feet a caress or disturbance in a far-off land. A Greek myth is,

you find, sweet on your tongue. Well done, my tourist, you've done it:
labelled the ideas in your head. I know them. Too well. They thump

on my pillow, there's more of them in the corridor. The holiday is
coming for me, too. And my lungs will be the same as yours.

Cliff / Boy

An artist said it first: now we've got photographs,
there is no need to copy nature. Photography freed them.
Technology freed them. I went to the cinema,
and now to call your body stone, or clay, or even try to
give you a colour is faking it, like pretending love.
The work is otherwiseness:

You stand tall without a sculptor;
crumble and no verse marks it.
Before 'a while' is too long, I want to see you again.
This summer. When I do, I'll remember that stories can be weak,
words weaker than weak. You don't need them,
can't hear them, will never hear them. Let's make it a date.

Planet introduces herself

Hi.
I, morning,
invented one morning.
Hello!
I, burgundy,
the colour of invention.
Hey. Invention,
a hound you wanted.
Another hound,
exhaling fatally.

I, fright.
An inkling, living on a fingertip.
I, the inkling,
a query breathing in.

Inklings, adding up:
the hounds dug out,
tellurian sockets peeled,
driven arteries cracked.

Bed rest

and a window
measured in metres.
Quite large enough.

Virginia Woolf and her
skies seen with ill eyes.
Thank you, V.

Can I call you V?
No-one else does.

The view from my face
no register, at first.

Growths and blots were
eventually chimneys.

Small pots assembled
and soldierly were,
eventually, orange.

No. (He holds a finger up).
Terracotta orange. The rain
did not escape me.

No inching water blade
(he tries at poetry).
I'm vigilant, me.

Noxious to you,
and the nurse.

I know it.
Is this self-awareness
self-improving?

Or is it just pointing?
My point is that a colour
was realised not seen.

There is no point when
the point is a splinter.

And yours, a needle,
hammer-sized,
sewing a wound.

Does a splinter
deserve a page?

Excuse me.
I have seen lies
burn in the sun.

Cybernated

What is happening?!
Can we all agree that
the inky headlands

which appear totally still
are really moving?
Everyone can reply
They move
as if drawn by horses
|
Yes! Curved and sandy
It's just hard to tell
under the city's headdress
|
I find them airless and pleasant
|
Yes, very pleasant
|
What is happening?!
Wanting a sea view so hard
I've found it in grit, in concrete,
in bricks. A thread
|
The unspooling of promise
A tantalising drip drip
|
of things you don't
need to know, from a source
|
You most certainly don't
|

Still you thirst. Drip drip
Everyone can reply
With silted fingertips
and lipstick
We can warm ourselves
in the blue glow of it

Make gifts like these
When waking up three hours
north of midnight is normal
and |
also | after | eventually | when |
We get back to normal
Poll
I've found sea views

in grit	42%
in concrete	12%
between bricks	46%

What is happening?!
Someone is nine hours north of you
Legs cool, energy-saved and grey-blue
A device waiting.

Midway through building a girl

Those are Cinder's shoes!
So small they can hide in other shoes.

A torso wide and bare,
the way Matisse saw them.

Help me choose an eye colour.
Bluish Black?

Put the clefts in. Unarguable creases.
A comma between her lips.

paint the room yellow because

yellow is like gold / but more athletic
acrobatic / really
don't rush please / lemon
butter / from straw to cake
biscuit between / cane and punch
consider / an outcry / a zing
it shoots in hats / and healing spices
turn to another colour / another vandal
this one / millennial chapel
it honeys your thoughts / i meant
rooms / you can paint the rooms / too.

IRL

In real life / Say it slowly /
Taller / Loller than I expected /
Memories don't rush / So there's no need to run /

Let's resist the writers / Cliche / Coffee shops / And men /

I don't resist / A fine-knuckled expresso / Espresso /

A body is more easily made of exes / Rarer, esses /

My favourite punch of time / When there are no clocks /
The childhoods we had render themselves again /
Ices lull when you're small /
Food lulls when you're that small /
Sweets are lies /

All else is true / My favourite lie is the future /
An unhandled punch of time / Sometimes called a daydream /

I can't be bothered / Filling in my gaps /
The gaps are melting /
Larger with time / Lulling pleasantly /
The gaps are killing pleasantly /

I suppose friends keep watch too

A kitchen. Cold flecks, cooling flecks, boiled eggs
that stay in their shells. A slow lid closing,
like days do. Her thoughts close. One by one,
they shutter as shops do.

A screen, and all the performances within.
She tries to keep up.
Tech is encouraging, like that.
It makes you try at it.

A swivel, and the detection of it under her skin.
The gaze is bigger than noise.
An anti-friend, vermicular,
in the machine.

"Your tears are tasty in my glass."
They talk, because they're familiar.
"It's a glass, now, is it?" A shop opens,
behind her brows and slightly above them.

Inside is a bellied, fizzy promise.
Night in the snip of two fingers.
"You're an algorithm." She wondered
if it could become a glass.

She doesn't have tears, but she can produce them.
"Happy birthday."
The worm remembered.
And it doesn't even like her.

There's a texture in her shadow.
Movement. Her phone,
chewing, irretrievably.
A bite of surveillance must be good.

Jealous

That full and flaunting novice
In student brown and cardigan
pink A flower bed across her
chest Her long future pulls to
the horizon It sears like a god.

Lethargy

Lie like a
cut worm

a dead emperor

an eyelid

lie like the face in
someone else's head
lie like

bark
the gaze on the bark

the unthinking thought on
the gaze on the bark.

Acknowledgments

We're surely in the place to remember start lines, and to stand by them as respectfully as we do headstones. The headstone and the most decisive starting point both have a finality about them, something in common: they only point you one way. But where are the starting blocks for poets? Where's the writer's checkered grid?

My start line is on the fifth floor of the Southbank Centre, in the Poetry Library. There's another inside the pages of Poetry London. I must reserve an early acknowledgement for an elixir: admiration. Often invisible. Exceeding the day-to-day so suddenly, it's almost extraterrestrial. I would tweet at poets after reading their work; hearing back from them was like hearing from a rock star. I read and admired Caroline Bird, Ramona Herdman, Daniel Poppick, John McCullough, and many others.

I must acknowledge David Hockney's body of work. Looking at his early-career canvases, painted in LA, is a reminder that an artist's materials change. A poet's materials change, too.

Finally, the wending of a universe made these poems possible. It includes Long Covid (and recovery). A room of my own. The girls I work with. And a publishing team following their hearts.

Some poems in this collection, or previous versions thereof, have appeared in the following publications:

41 years old and reading Mr Men - *Porridge*

41 years old and reading Mr Men - *Pissour, Salò Press*

I've seen Mikaela - *Pissour, Salò Press*

Bed rest - *Pissour, Salò Press*

Lethargy - *Seaford Review*

Stupdendous Ruler Painter - *Frazzled Lit*

When a Man Washes In - *tiny wren lit*

How to turn one villian into two - *Dust Poetry*

Founded in Atlanta, Georgia in 2023, PARLYAREE PRESS is dedicated to publishing writing that expands, reveals, and interrogates the mainstream. We seek out fiction, creative nonfiction, and poetry that exists in the liminal space between what was and what will be.

The cant of circus performers, freaks, queers, and thespians, Parlyaree is the invented language required to tell the stories of those othered, to keep their secrets, to keep them safe. It is a polyglot of experiences that may only be told in one's own voice. Parlyaree—as an invented language—borrows from what was to create something new.

That is what excites us at Parlyaree Press. Stories that transform; essays that reimagine; poetry that takes us behind the stanza to the core of our being and back again; language that plays as much as it conveys.

Writers: tell us your secrets.
Readers: reimagine your worlds.

www.ingramcontent.com/pod-product-compliance
Lightning Source LLC
LaVergne TN
LVHW031607060526
838201LV00063B/4768